ACHIEVE LEVEL 5

SCIENCE

By Gerald Page

RISING STARS

Rising Stars UK Ltd., 22 Grafton Street, London W1S 4EX

www.risingstars-uk.com

Every effort has been made to trace copyright holders and obtain their permission for the use of copyright material. The authors and publishers will gladly receive information enabling them to rectify any error or omission in subsequent editions.

All facts are correct at time of going to press.

This edition 2005
Reprinted 2006, 2007

Educational consultants: Robert McCorkell and Louise Moore
Cover design: Burville Riley
Design: Branford Graphics
Illustrations: Burville Riley, Beehive Illustration (Theresa Tibbetts), Jim Eldridge and Oxford Designers and Illustrators
Cover image: Beehive Illustration (Theresa Tibbetts)

British Library Cataloguing in Publication Data
A CIP record for this book is available from the British Library.

ISBN 978 1 905056 10 1

Printed by Craft Print International Ltd, Singapore

Contents

How to use this book   4

The National Tests   6

Test tips and technique   8

Section 1:   Level 4 —   The Tricky Bits   10

Section 2:   Level 5 —   Life processes and living things   20
                         Materials and their properties   31
                         Physical processes   41
                         Scientific enquiry   51
                         Handling data   55

Section 3:   Key facts   57

Answers   61

How to use this book

(1) **Introduction** – This section tells you what you need to do to achieve a Level 5. It picks out the key learning objective and explains it simply to you.

(2) **Self-assessment** – Colour in the face that best describes your understanding of this concept.

(3) **Question** – The question helps you to learn by doing. It is presented in a similar way to a SATs question and gives you a real example to work with.

(4) **Flow chart** – This shows you the steps to use when completing questions like this. Some of the advice appears on every flow chart, such as 'Read the question then read it again'.

 This icon indicates the section is a *teaching* section.

(5) **Tip boxes** – These provide test hints and general tips on getting the best marks in the tests.

WHAT WE HAVE INCLUDED:

★ Those topics at Level 4 that are trickiest to get right.

★ ALL Level 5 content so you know that you are covering all the topics that could come up in the test.

★ We have also put in a big selection of our favourite test techniques, tips for revision and some advice on what the tests are all about, as well as the answers so you can see how well you are getting on.

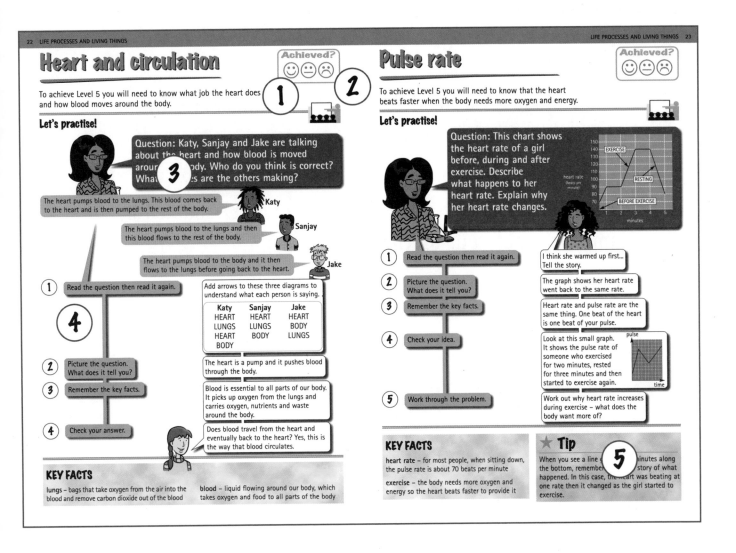

Heart and circulation

Achieved? 😊 😐 ☹ ①

To achieve Level 5 you will need to know what job the heart does and how blood moves around the body.

Let's practise!

Question: Katy, Sanjay and Jake are talking about the heart and how blood is moved around the body. Who do you think is correct? What mistakes are the others making? ③

The heart pumps blood to the lungs. This blood comes back to the heart and is then pumped to the rest of the body. — **Katy**

The heart pumps blood to the lungs and then this blood flows to the rest of the body. — **Sanjay**

The heart pumps blood to the body and it then flows to the lungs before going back to the heart. — **Jake**

① Read the question then read it again.

④

Add arrows to these three diagrams to understand what each person is saying.

Katy	Sanjay	Jake
HEART	HEART	HEART
LUNGS	LUNGS	BODY
HEART	BODY	LUNGS
BODY		

The heart is a pump and it pushes blood through the body.

② Picture the question. What does it tell you?

③ Remember the key facts.

Blood is essential to all parts of our body. It picks up oxygen from the lungs and carries oxygen, nutrients and waste around the body.

④ Check your answer.

Does blood travel from the heart and eventually back to the heart? Yes, this is the way that blood circulates.

KEY FACTS

lungs – bags that take oxygen from the air into the blood and remove carbon dioxide out of the blood

blood – liquid flowing around our body, which takes oxygen and food to all parts of the body

---

Pulse rate

Achieved? 😊 😐 ☹ ②

To achieve Level 5 you will need to know that the heart beats faster when the body needs more oxygen and energy.

Let's practise!

Question: This chart shows the heart rate of a girl before, during and after exercise. Describe what happens to her heart rate. Explain why her heart rate changes.

[Graph: heart rate (beats per minute) vs minutes, showing EXERCISE, RESTING, BEFORE EXERCISE]

① Read the question then read it again.

I think she warmed up first… Tell the story.

② Picture the question. What does it tell you?

The graph shows her heart rate went back to the same rate.

③ Remember the key facts.

Heart rate and pulse rate are the same thing. One beat of the heart is one beat of your pulse.

④ Check your idea.

Look at this small graph. It shows the pulse rate of someone who exercised for two minutes, rested for three minutes and then started to exercise again.

[small graph: pulse vs time]

⑤ Work through the problem.

Work out why heart rate increases during exercise – what does the body want more of?

KEY FACTS

heart rate – for most people, when sitting down, the pulse rate is about 70 beats per minute

exercise – the body needs more oxygen and energy so the heart beats faster to provide it

★ Tip

⑤

When you see a line graph with minutes along the bottom, remember it's a story of what happened. In this case, the heart was beating at one rate then it changed as the girl started to exercise.

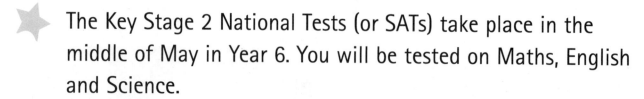

The National Tests

Key facts

⭐ The Key Stage 2 National Tests (or SATs) take place in the middle of May in Year 6. You will be tested on Maths, English and Science.

⭐ The tests take place in your school and will be marked by examiners – not your teacher!

⭐ You will get your results in July, two months after you take the tests.

⭐ Individual test scores are not made public, but a school's combined scores are published in what are commonly known as league tables.

The Science National Tests

You will take two tests in Science each one lasting 45 minutes. These are designed to test your knowledge and skills across the following areas of Science:

● Life processes and living things – the human body, plants and animals and their habitats.

● Materials and their properties – changing different materials, understanding the characteristics of different materials.

● Physical processes – electricity, forces, light and sound, the Sun and the Earth.

● Scientific enquiry – ideas and evidence about Science and investigative skills.

DON'T FORGET!

Scientific Enquiry – The National Tests now include more questions that test your *Scientific Enquiry* skills.

The questions will often be based around a picture or a description of an investigation that children have carried out, along with their results. You won't need to carry out the investigation in the test but you might be asked how you would improve it if you were doing the investigation in class.

Recent National Tests papers included questions like:

- Write the question that children were investigating.
- Choose the correct equipment to use in an investigation.
- Complete a table of results from an investigation.
- Draw conclusions from the results of investigations.
- Answer questions about graphs and charts completed in an investigation.
- Describe what children have found out from an investigation.

You might also have to answer some questions about a famous scientist! In 2003 there was a series of questions about Edward Jenner. He found a cure for smallpox a long time ago and saved millions of lives!

Test tips and technique

Before the test

1 When you revise, try revising a 'little and often' rather than in long sessions.

2 Learn the Key Facts (at the end of the book) so that you can recall them instantly. These are your tools for performing your calculations.

3 Revise with a friend. You can encourage and learn from each other.

4 Get a good night's sleep the night before.

5 Make sure you have breakfast!

6 Be prepared – bring your own pens and pencils and wear a watch to check the time as you go.

During the test

1 Don't rush the first few questions. These tend to be quite straightforward, so don't make any silly mistakes.

2 As you know by now, READ THE QUESTION THEN READ IT AGAIN.

3 If you get stuck, don't linger on the same question – move on! You can come back to it later.

4 Never leave a multiple choice question. Guess if you really can't work out the answer.

5 Check to see how many marks a question is worth. Have you 'earned' those marks with your answer?

6 Check your answers after each question. Does your answer look correct?

7 Be aware of the time. After 20 minutes, check to see how far you have got.

8 Try to leave a couple of minutes at the end to read through what you have written.

9 Don't leave any questions unanswered. In the two minutes you have left yourself at the end, make an educated guess at the questions you really couldn't do.

10 Remember, as long as you have done your best, nobody can ask for more. Only you will know if that is the case.

Things to remember

1 Don't panic! If you see a difficult question, take your time, re-read it and have a go!

2 Check every question and every page to be sure you don't miss any! Some questions will want two answers.

3 If a question is about measuring, always write in the UNIT of MEASUREMENT (e.g. newtons, l, kg).

4 Don't be afraid to ask a teacher for anything you need, such as tracing paper or another pencil.

5 Write neatly – if you want to change an answer, put a line through it and write beside the answer box.

6 Always double-check your answers.

Good luck!

Roots, stems and water

At Level 4 you should be able to say how different parts of a plant work.
For example: all plants need water. Water is drawn up from the roots and travels to all parts of the plant through the stem.

Let's practise!

Question: Jim grew 20 bean seeds until they were 6 cm tall. He gently took them out of the compost, leaving the roots intact. He left five with all of their roots, cut a small amount from the next five, took most of the roots off the next five shoots and completely removed the roots from the last five. What do you think happened to each of the seedlings when he replanted them?

a) Which seedlings would you expect to die?
b) Which would grow best?

 Read the question then read it again.

The question is asking about the effect removing roots has.

 Picture the experiment.

Jim took care to lift the seedlings without damaging the roots.

 Study the question and make sense of it.

Even though Jim didn't cut any roots off 5 seedlings, he still pulled them up. That makes it easier to compare the effect.

 Remember the key facts.

What is the function of roots? What effect will cutting them off have?

KEY FACTS

water – all living things need it

roots – take water from the soil

stems – water travels up stems from roots

leaves and flowers – need water, which travels up to them

★ Tip

Gardeners often replant seedlings, but always try not to damage the roots. Only people who grow miniature trees (bonsai) cut roots to slow down the plant's growth.

Thermal insulators and conductors

Achieved?

At Level 4 you are expected to know that heat passes through some materials more easily than through others.
For example: heat travels more easily through metals than it does through plastic and wood.

Let's practise!

Experiment: Jo puts a metal mass, a piece of polystyrene and a plastic car on a radiator. She waits 10 minutes.
- The metal mass feels hot.
- The plastic car feels warm.
- The polystyrene is not warm.

Why is there a difference in the heat of the materials?

1. Read the question then read it again.
2. Picture the question. What can you work out?
3. Think about real life examples.
4. Remember the key facts.
5. Work through the problem.

Why is one material hotter than the others?

The heat must have come from the radiator and pass through the materials.

Kettles and pans have plastic or wooden handles so they are not hot to the touch. Pans are metal so heat can travel to the food quickly.

Heat travels through materials.

Heat must travel through the metal mass and plastic car. If it can travel easily through a material then that material is a good conductor.

KEY FACTS

material – what objects are made from

metals – good conductors of heat

plastics – poor conductors of heat

wood – a very poor conductor of heat

CHECK YOUR ANSWER

- A conductor of electricity lets electricity through.
- A conductor of heat lets heat through.
- Good thermal conductors let heat through more easily than poor thermal conductors.

Separating mixtures

Achieved?

At Level 4 you will need to know about the ways to separate simple mixtures.
For example: a sugar and water solution.

Let's practise!

Experiment: Let's make sugar crystals using the following method.

1. Read the question then read it again.

2. Think about the question. What do you know?

3. Remember the key facts.

4. Work through the problem.

We start with a concentrated solution of sugar and water.

If we pour a solution of sugar and water through a sieve, nothing useful happens. The solution simply goes through the sieve.

Sugar dissolves in water. If we let the water evaporate, the sugar will be left behind.

Will evaporating the water quickly give big crystals or will it be better to do it slowly?

KEY FACTS

dissolve – a solid splits into tiny particles in water

solution – a mixture where a solid has dissolved in a liquid

evaporate – this happens when a liquid turns to a gas. This leaves behind any solid that was dissolved

concentrated solution – a solution with a lot of solid dissolved in the liquid

Ways to separate mixtures:

sieve – use this to separate most undissolved solids from a liquid, or to separate two solids of different sizes

filter – use this to separate a solution from tiny undissolved pieces

Friction

To reach Level 4 you need to know that forces can stop objects moving.
For example: friction can stop cars that are on a slope from rolling.

Let's practise!

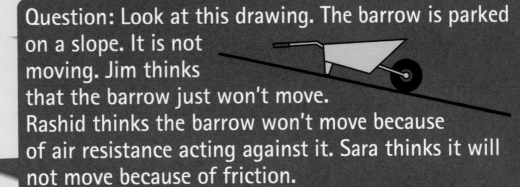

Question: Look at this drawing. The barrow is parked on a slope. It is not moving. Jim thinks that the barrow just won't move. Rashid thinks the barrow won't move because of air resistance acting against it. Sara thinks it will not move because of friction.
- ● Who do you think is correct?
- ● Why do you think this?

1 Read the question then read it again.

The barrow is not moving because a force is stopping it.

2 Picture the question. Try it out.

Put an object on a book and tilt the book. The object begins to slide once the slope is steep enough.

3 Think of an everyday example.

When a barrow is parked on a slope, it is the friction between the wheel and axle, and between the feet and the ground, that stops it moving.

4 Work through the problem.

Gravity is pulling the barrow down the slope. What force is working against gravity? It cannot be air resistance because air resistance only works when something is moving.

KEY FACTS

gravity – the force that pulls all objects towards the Earth

friction – the force between two surfaces. It stops things moving or slows down their movement

air resistance – the force that slows objects as they move through the air

★ Tip

The barrow will move once the slope is steep enough. If the axle is rusty there will more friction so it will not roll so easily.

Magnetic attraction and repulsion

Achieved?

At Level 4 you will need to know that magnetic force attracts steel objects like compass needles.

Let's practise!

Experiment: Peter had three bar magnets. He thought the biggest would be stronger than the smallest. He set up a test. He measured the distance each magnet was from a compass to make the needle swing. He noticed one end of the compass was attracted to the red end of the magnet.
Explain how Peter's test worked.

1 Read the question then read it again.

Notice that one end of the compass needle was attracted by one end of the magnet.

2 Picture the question. What does it tell you?

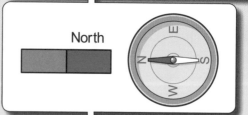
North

3 Think about magnetic poles.

Think about magnetic poles. The magnetic force is stronger at the end of the magnet – these ends are called poles.

4 Remember the key facts.

Like poles repel and unlike poles attract.

5 Work through the problem.

The needle moves very easily when the magnet is near. It attracts or repels the needle.

 Tip

Always use the correct words when talking about magnets:
Poles are the ends of the magnet.
Attract is the correct word. Do not say 'stick'.
Repel is the correct word for 'push apart'.

KEY FACTS

A compass needle is just like a bar magnet, with a south and a north pole.

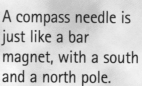

Magnetic sorting

At Level 4 you will need to know which metals are magnetic
and which are not.

Let's practise!

Question: Ravi tests materials to see which are attracted to a
magnet. He sorts them into two sets.
All the materials are metal and some are magnetic.
He lists the different metals.

Metal	Used for	Does it conduct electricity?	Is it attracted to magnets?
aluminium	many pans	yes	no
steel	scissors	yes	yes
brass	old bells	yes	no
silver	rings	yes	no
iron	nails	yes	yes

List the metals that are magnetic and the metals that are
not magnetic.

Metals attracted to magnets	Metals not attracted to magnets

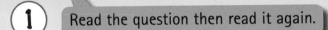

1 Read the question then read it again.

No non-metals are magnetic. Some
metals are attracted to magnets.

2 Picture the question. What does it
tell you?

All you have to do is write two lists.

3 Think of an everyday example.

Iron and its alloy steel are the only
magnetic metals shown on the list.

4 Work through the problem.

HINTS

- When testing metals, if one is attracted to a magnet, it must have iron or steel
in it. Tin cans only have a very thin layer of tin over an inside of steel.

- Find out as much as you can about types of metals and what they are used for.

Patterns in data

At Level 4 you will need to be able to interpret patterns in data.
For example: interpreting a pie chart.

Let's practise!

Experiment: This pie chart shows the eye colour of children in Class 5.

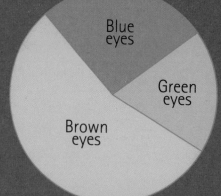

Blue eyes

Green eyes

Brown eyes

Which was the most common eye colour?
Which eye colour did more than one-quarter but less than half of the children have?

1 Read the question then read it again.

2 Picture the question. What does it tell you?

3 Remember the key facts.

4 Work through the problem.

You are only being asked to say what the chart shows.

The whole class is shown by the circle. The parts are shown by the slices.

The biggest slice shows most children.

We can see that green eyes are least common and brown eyes are most common.

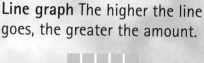

KEY FACTS

There are three main types of graphs and charts.

Bar chart The taller the column, the greater the amount.

Pie chart The bigger the piece of pie, the greater the amount.

Line graph The higher the line goes, the greater the amount.

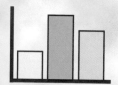

Explaining patterns in data

Achieved?

At Level 4 you will need to be able to explain patterns in data.
For example: explaining why one factor depends on another.

Let's practise!

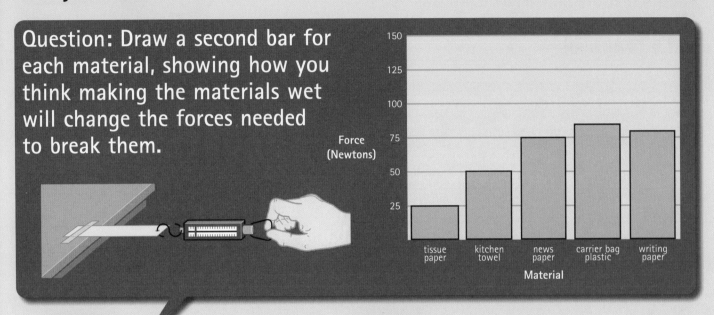

Question: Draw a second bar for each material, showing how you think making the materials wet will change the forces needed to break them.

Force (Newtons) — axis values: 150, 125, 100, 75, 50, 25

Materials: tissue paper, kitchen towel, news paper, carrier bag plastic, writing paper

Material

(1) Read the question then read it again.

(2) Picture the question. What does it tell you?

(3) Remember the key facts.

(4) Work through the problem.

The strips are all different materials.

The strips should be the same size.

Some papers are very weak when wet. Plastic will not soak up water.

Most of the materials will be weaker when damp, but we must use the same amount of water on each.

★ Tip

Look for the patterns and describe them first. If there is a change in the pattern, think of a reason why the change could have happened.

Scientific enquiry – spotting problem results

Achieved?

To reach Level 4 you will need to be able to spot results that are probably wrong.

Let's practise!

Experiment: Jim and Sue were seeing how high different balls bounce.
They measured the bounce of each ball.
Each one was dropped from the same height.
a) Explain the pattern of most of the results.
b) Circle the one result which was probably a mistake.
c) Explain why you think it is a mistake.

Type of ball	How high the ball bounced		
	1st try	2nd try	3rd try
tennis	30	34	56
golf	41	40	38
ping pong	62	60	59

1 Read the question then read it again.

You have to explain the pattern.
In a), this means you will have to say which was the bounciest ball.
You only need to circle one result in question b).

2 Picture the question.

Look at the pattern of the results – you would expect similar results on each try.

3 Remember the key facts.

Distance bounced depends on the type of ball.

4 Work through the problem.

The pattern of the results shows that the ping pong ball is the best bouncer.
The mistake was the 56 cm result.
It was much higher than the other results for the same ball. It was further than the golf ball.

KEY FACTS

pattern – look for a sequence of results.
Look for increases or decreases

Scientific enquiry – variables

To reach Level 4 you will need to be able to say which variables you will change, which you will measure and which you will keep the same.

Let's practise!

Shefqat is seeing how tall bean and pea seedlings grow after 10 days.	Julie is seeing how various exercises affect her pulse rate.	Tim is doing an experiment to see if the number of times he stirs the water affects the speed at which salt dissolves.
Circle the variables that you would keep the same in this experiment.	Circle the variables that you would alter in this experiment.	Circle the variables that you would measure in this experiment.
Variables ● the compost ● height of seedling ● the temperature ● the type of seed	**Variables** ● Julie's pulse rate ● the type of exercise she does ● how she measures her pulse rate	**Variables** ● the number of stirs ● the time taken to dissolve ● the amount of salt at the start

1 Read the question then read it again.

2 Remember the key facts.

The words are really important here.

What you keep the same are the variables that you do not want to affect your measurements. In most experiments, you try to alter only one thing at a time and then try to measure the changes that occur.

3 Work through the problem.

| For Shefqat's experiment you circle 'compost' and 'temperature' because those two factors should be the same for each type of seed to ensure the test is fair. | For Julie's experiment you circle the 'type of exercise' because she wants to see how this single factor affects her pulse rate. It doesn't matter how she measures her pulse rate, so long as as it is accurate. | For Tim's experiment you circle them all. He wants to measure the thing that has the effect (the number of stirs) and what effect it has (time taken to dissolve). He will need to check that the amount of salt at the start is the same. |

Function of human organs

Achieved?

To achieve Level 5 you will need to know the main functions of human organs.
For example: the heart, lungs and stomach functions.

Let's practise!

Question: What are the main functions of the heart, the lungs and the stomach?

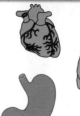

heart	
lungs	
stomach	

① Read the question then read it again.

② Picture the human body.

③ Study the question and make sense of it.

④ Remember the key facts.

⑤ Work through the problem.

⑥ Check your answer.

'Function' means the job something does. An organ is part of the body with a special job to do.

Think about where these organs are located.

The lungs and heart are very close to each other.

- The lungs are where gases are exchanged between the air and the body.
- The heart pumps blood.
- The stomach helps to digest food.

List the functions next to the name of the organ.

Use the word **pump** to describe the heart.

KEY FACTS

blood – liquid that carries food, waste and oxygen around the body
air – mixture of gases that we breathe
oxygen – the gas in air that our bodies need
carbon dioxide – the gas we breathe out

Plant organs

To achieve Level 5 you will need to know the main functions of plant organs.
For example: the reproductive parts of a flower.

Let's practise!

Question: What are the main organs of a flowering plant and what are their functions?

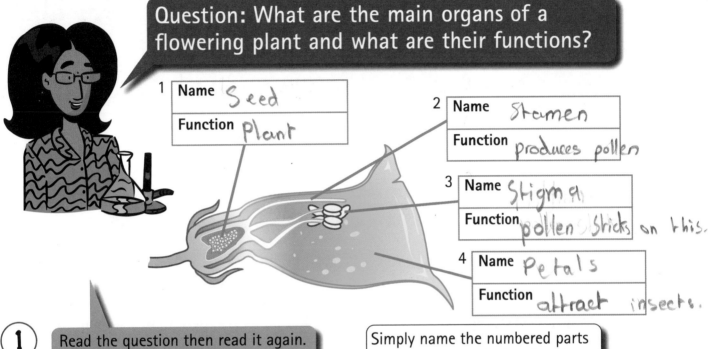

1 Name *Seed*
Function *Plant*

2 Name *Stamen*
Function *produces pollen*

3 Name *Stigma*
Function *pollen sticks on this.*

4 Name *Petals*
Function *attract insects.*

1 Read the question then read it again.

Simply name the numbered parts and say what their functions are.

2 Picture the question. What does it tell you?

These are the same organs as at Level 4, but this time you need to say what each one does.

3 Remember the key facts.

Flowers are there to produce seeds. Seeds develop from ovules in the ovary. Seeds are pollinated when male pollen from the stamen lands on the stigma. The pollen travels down to the ovules to make seeds.

4 Work through the problem.

Start by deciding which parts are male and which are female.

KEY FACTS

stigma – the female part where pollen sticks
stamen – the male parts, which produce pollen
ovule – undeveloped seed

ovary – the box that contains the ovule and later the seeds
seed – an object produced by a plant, which may eventually grow into another plant
petals – colourful outer part of flower

★ **Tip**

StigMA is female
StaMEN is male

Heart and circulation

To achieve Level 5 you will need to know what job the heart does and how blood moves around the body.

Let's practise!

Question: Katy, Sanjay and Jake are talking about the heart and how blood is moved around the body. Who do you think is correct? What mistakes are the others making?

The heart pumps blood to the lungs. This blood comes back to the heart and is then pumped to the rest of the body.

Katy

The heart pumps blood to the lungs and then this blood flows to the rest of the body.

Sanjay forgot the blood going 2nd time into h...

The heart pumps blood to the body and it then flows to the lungs before going back to the heart.

Jake put it the wrong way round

① Read the question then read it again.

Add arrows to these three diagrams to understand what each person is saying.

Katy	Sanjay	Jake
HEART	HEART	HEART
LUNGS	LUNGS	BODY
HEART	BODY	LUNGS
BODY		

② Picture the question. What does it tell you?

The heart is a pump and it pushes blood through the body.

③ Remember the key facts.

Blood is essential to all parts of our body. It picks up oxygen from the lungs and carries oxygen, nutrients and waste around the body.

④ Check your answer.

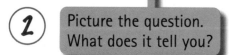

Does blood travel from the heart and eventually back to the heart? Yes, this is the way that blood circulates.

KEY FACTS

lungs – bags that take oxygen from the air into the blood and remove carbon dioxide out of the blood

blood – liquid flowing around our body, which takes oxygen and food to all parts of the body

Pulse rate

To achieve Level 5 you will need to know that the heart beats faster when the body needs more oxygen and energy.

Let's practise!

Question: This chart shows the heart rate of a girl before, during and after exercise. Describe what happens to her heart rate. Explain why her heart rate changes.

Her muscles need air and blood so to work faster it needs to more blood.

heart rate (beats per minute)

EXERCISE

RESTING

BEFORE EXERCISE

minutes

① Read the question then read it again.

I think she warmed up first... Tell the story.

② Picture the question. What does it tell you?

The graph shows her heart rate went back to the same rate.

③ Remember the key facts.

Heart rate and pulse rate are the same thing. One beat of the heart is one beat of your pulse.

④ Check your idea.

Look at this small graph. It shows the pulse rate of someone who exercised for two minutes, rested for three minutes and then started to exercise again.

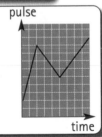

pulse

time

⑤ Work through the problem.

Work out why heart rate increases during exercise – what does the body want more of?

KEY FACTS

heart rate – for most people, when sitting down, the pulse rate is about 70 beats per minute

exercise – the body needs more oxygen and energy so the heart beats faster to provide it

★ Tip

When you see a line graph with minutes along the bottom, remember to tell the story of what happened. In this case, the heart was beating at one rate then it changed as the girl started to exercise.

Animal life cycles

To achieve Level 5 you will need to know the life cycles of different animals.

For example: the changes in an insect as it develops.

Let's practise!

Question: Describe the main parts of the life cycle of a house fly.

1 Read the question then read it again.

First, list the stages in the life cycle of a fly and then describe each one.

2 Picture the question. What does it tell you?

Draw each stage in a circle with arrows connecting the stages.

3 Remember the key facts.

Study the stages in the life cycle of different animals, such as frogs and flies. How are humans and other mammals different or similar?

4 Work through the problem.

All animals are born and grow old and die. They all go through stages. In humans and other mammals, several of the stages happen inside the mother's body before birth.

5 Check your answer.

When you have written the names of the stages, write in what happens at each stage.

KEY FACTS

egg – all animals start as eggs. You started as an egg inside your mother

maggot – in flies the egg hatches into a **maggot**. Maggots are like miniature eating machines! A maggot is like a **caterpillar stage in butterfly life cycles**

pupa – the maggot makes a covering around itself while it changes into an adult **fly**

adult – at this stage the fly mates, lays eggs and dies

 Tip

The frog life cycle is similar to the butterfly in many ways, but it does not make a pupa.

In mammals the young is born looking like a very small adult.

Plant life cycles

To achieve Level 5 you will need to know the main stages in a plant's life cycle.
For example: the stages of pollination and seed dispersal.

Let's practise!

Question: These stages in the life cycle of a flowering plant are mixed up. Number them in the correct order starting with germination.

- growing plant   `2`
- dispersal of seeds   `6`
- flowering   `3`

- development of seeds   `5`
- pollination   `4`
- germination of seed   `1`

(1) Read the question then read it again.

(2) Picture the question.
Think about what you know.

(3) Remember the key facts.

(4) Check your answer.

Decide where to start from. It is probably best to start with germination.

The cycle of a plant is similar to that of an animal. It grows, gets fertilised, produces seeds and dies.

Pollination and germination are two different processes. Pollination happens when male pollen meets the female ovule and makes a seed.

Read through the list – picture each stage and what went before.

KEY FACTS

pollination – the process where pollen from the male part of the plant fertilises the female ovule to make a seed

germination – the process where a seed starts growing into a plant

★ Tip

Think about a particular flower, such as a dandelion. You see the bright yellow flower before the fluffy seeds are formed. This attracts insects for pollination.

Keys

To achieve Level 5 you will need to be able to work out the names of living things using keys.

Let's practise!

Question: Name the twigs A and B.

A
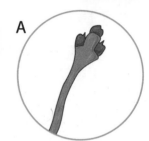

B
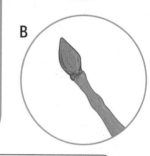

Is there a single bud?

yes
Are the buds large and green?

no
Are the buds in groups at the end of the twig?

yes
chestnut B

no
ash

yes
oak A

no
lime

① Read the question then read it again.

You probably do not know the answer straight away, so try to work it out logically. Look at the twig labelled A. Answer the questions in the key based on that twig.

② Picture the question.

Start at the beginning. Answer the first question in the sequence. There are two pathways. Choose the answers that match twig A.

③ Remember the key facts.

Buds opposite each other are in pairs on either side of the twig.

④ Check your answer.

Now answer the questions based on twig B. You should end up with a different answer from twig A.

KEY FACTS

twig – thin part at the end part of a branch
bud – tightly folded leaves and flowers. In winter these are protected by bud scales

Buds are often set out in pairs opposite each other down the twig. There is usually a single bud at the very end of the twig.

★ Tip

All keys work like this one. Once you understand this one you will be able to use most keys.

Classification

To achieve Level 5 you will need to classify living things into groups.
For example: animals with backbones.

Let's practise!

Question: Draw a line from each animal group to its description.

- mammal — has damp skin and lays eggs in water
- bird — has dry scaly skin and lays eggs on land
- reptile — has feathers and lays eggs
- amphibian — lives in water and has gills
- fish — gives birth to live young and feeds young on milk

List these animals and say which group each one belongs to.

swallow   alligator   newt   kangaroo   lizard
Bird   *reptile*   *amphibian*   *mammal*   *reptile*
whale   toad   sparrow   stickleback   cod
mammal   *amphibian*   *bird*   *fish*   *fish*

(Clue: there are two of each kind.)

1 Read the question then read it again.

Start to put the animals in pairs that seem similar.

2 Picture the question. What do you know?

Read about each kind of animal and think about the skin each has. Fish can be tricky as some are scaly and some are not. Mammals can be difficult as some appear hairy and others do not.

3 Remember the key facts.

These are all in the question – the description of each animal type.

4 Work through the problem.

If you end up with three in one group, one of them must be wrong.

5 Check your answer.

Think of another example of each animal type.

KEY FACTS – the language

eggs – birds have hard eggs, reptiles have leathery eggs and amphibians and fish have soft, squishy eggs

hair – mammals, like humans, only have noticeable hair on a few parts of their body. Whales do not appear to have hair

scales – made of a material like your fingernail

Habitats

To achieve Level 5 you will need to know the ways in which animals and plants are suited to different habitats. For example: the things you would need to provide in a tank of slugs, snails and worms.

Let's practise!

Question: Kate wants to use an old fish tank to make a great habitat for lots of animals to live in. What does she need to make it a place for worms? What sort of food would slugs and snails like? What would spiders need in order to feel at home? What should she put in the tank for woodlice?

(1) Read the question then read it again.

You need to think about the environment and food each type of animal likes.

(2) Picture the question. What does it tell you?

Worms need soil, but you need to say if the soil needs to be damp or dry.

(3) Remember the key facts.

Spiders are the only carnivores – they catch flies and will need somewhere to hang their webs.

(4) Check your answer.

Plan a home for woodlice in your classroom. What things would you need to provide for them?

Mud, stones, twigs.

KEY FACTS

habitat – the place where an animal or plant lives

environment – what the conditions in a habitat are like

conditions – what a place is like. Is it damp or dry? Is it hot or cold?

★ Tip

All animals and plants live in habitats that suit them. If the conditions do not give them what they need, they will die.

A bird's habitat might be gardens or woods. Just because birds spend a lot of time in their nest does not mean that their nest is their habitat.

Environments

To achieve Level 5 you will need to know the ways that some animals and plants are suited to their environment.

For example: some plants have a number of ways of conserving water.

Let's practise!

> Question: Look at this cactus plant. In what ways is it suited to its environment? Finish off the sentences with one of these endings:
>
> water evaporating   make food
>
> store water   water from the soil
>
> animals eating the plant

(Cactus diagram labels: spikes, tough outer skin, swollen stems, green stem, deep roots)

Tough outer skin to stop **Water evaporating** plant.

Spikes to stop **animals eating the plant**

Green stem to **Make food**

Swollen stems to **Store water**

Deep roots to get **Water from the soil**

1 Read the question then read it again.

Think about a cactus and the way it survives in the desert.

2 Picture the question. What does it tell you?

The endings can only be used once. Some could fit in more than one place but there is one solution that works best.

3 Remember the key facts.

Cacti need to store water. They need to avoid losing water. They need to stop animals from eating them.

4 Think about another example.

How are worms suited to their environment? They have a long thin body, they are slimy to slide through the soil and they eat decaying plants in the soil.

KEY FACTS

environment – what a place is like

food – plants normally make food in their leaves. Cacti use their green stems to make food

Competition for light and water

To achieve Level 5 you will need to show you understand how plants and animals get enough light and water to grow and breed.

Let's practise!

Question: Deciduous trees do not have leaves in winter and only small, new leaves in spring. In a deciduous wood in spring the ground is covered with many small flowers. In summer these plants die down and there is mainly bare ground. Now think about evergreen trees. The ground is bare all year.
Why is this?

1 Read the question then read it again.

The question is asking about the reason why small plants only grow under trees in spring. Why is it different under evergreen trees?

2 Picture the question. What does it tell you?

In spring, there are only small, new leaves on the deciduous trees. It is always dark under evergreen trees.

3 Remember the key facts.

Flowers would not get enough light in the summer because of the shade of the tree. They don't grow under evergreens.

4 Think of other examples like this.

In the spring, bulbs such as daffodils grow in grass. Once the grass starts to grow the daffodils wither and shrink until next spring.

KEY FACTS

deciduous – plants that lose their leaves

evergreen – plants, like conifers, that keep their leaves all year

bulbs – stores of energy that let a plant start growing

★ Tip

You do not need to know much about plants to work this one out. It is all about one type of plant starting to grow before the others have woken up. They can only do this with a ready-made food store. They use their leaves to refill their food store just before the other plants overgrow them.

Burning

To achieve Level 5 you will need to know that some materials burn when they are heated.
For example: some materials only melt, while others melt and then burn. Another group burns without melting.

Let's practise!

Question: Tan's teacher heated different materials over a candle flame.

wood   bread   wool   chocolate   salt

The class put them into three different groups:

Melt then burn   Burn without melting   No change

Which group will you put each material into?

Melt then burn	Burn without melting	No change

① Read the question then read it again.

Look at each material and decide what would happen to it.

② Think of everyday examples.

If the oven is too hot, a cake will overcook and become black and burnt. If you heat marshmallows on a barbecue, they go drippy and will burn if they fall into the fire.

③ Work through the problem.

Which materials will not change?

KEY FACTS

melt – turn from a solid into a liquid

burn – catch fire and combine with oxygen in the air

★ Tip

When a material burns it produces new materials. Toast that burns turns into black carbon. The smoke that comes off burning toast is a new material, too.

Fizzing mixtures

Achieved?

To achieve Level 5 you will need to know that some mixtures produce gas.
For example: vinegar and baking powder produce a gas when they are mixed.

Let's practise!

Question: Andy's teacher had two small bottles. He put water and salt into one of the bottles. After a short time the salt disappeared. He put vinegar and baking powder into the other bottle. The mixture fizzed and bubbled.

- What happened to the salt in the water?
- Why do you think the second mixture fizzed and bubbled?
- Which of the two changes would be most difficult to reverse?

1 Read the question then read it again.

Think about the changes that made the second mixture fizz and bubble. The first mixture is much simpler – the salt dissolved in the water.

2 What is similar in everyday life?

To make cakes we add baking powder to our mix. This makes bubbles, which get bigger in the oven and make the cake light and fluffy. Yeast makes bubbles in bread dough, which makes the holes in bread. Salt dissolves in water.

3 Remember the key facts.

There is a change happening in the bubbling mixture that is very difficult to reverse. The chemical reaction between the baking powder and the vinegar produces a gas called carbon dioxide.

KEY FACTS

reversible change – a change that can be easily reversed

dissolving – when a solid disappears into a liquid, like salt in water

vinegar – this is an acid

★ Tip

Try adding baking powder to water and see what happens.

Evaporation

To achieve Level 5 you will need to know that evaporation takes place in a variety of conditions.
For example: moving air increases the speed of evaporation.

Let's practise!

Question: Kamal put 100 ml of water into each of three identical jars. He put a big battery fan, a small battery fan near another and no fan near the third.

3 hours later he checked how much water was in each jar.
What happened to the water?
Explain why some jars had less water in than others.

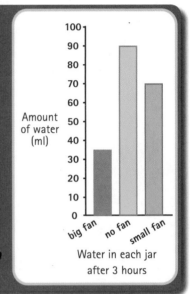

Amount of water (ml)

100
90
80
70
60
50
40
30
20
10
0

big fan   no fan   small fan

Water in each jar
after 3 hours

1 Read the question then read it again.

2 Picture the question.
What can you work out?

3 Remember the key facts.

4 Work through the problem.

Each jar started with the same amount of water (100 ml). After a time some of the water in each jar had gone.

Water has turned to a gas and gone into the air.

When a liquid turns to gas it is called evaporation.

Why did more water evaporate from one container than another? Moving air blew away water vapour near the surface of the jar so more water evaporated.

KEY FACTS

evaporate – turn from a liquid to a gas

★ Tip

Liquids evaporate more quickly when:

- they are warmed
- there is a breeze blowing over the top of them

Condensation

To achieve Level 5 you will need to know the conditions in which condensation takes place.
For example: the water vapour in air condenses on cold surfaces.

Let's practise!

Question: Lee took one can of drink out of the fridge. He took a similar can from the cupboard. He did not open either can. Soon after he put them on the table, water was running down the outside of the can from the fridge but not down the can from the cupboard.

Explain why there was water on the can from the fridge. Why was there a difference between the cans?

1 Read the question then read it again.

Something was happening on the cold can.

2 Picture the question. What can you work out?

The water must have come from the air.

3 Think of similar examples.

When you breathe on a mirror, it mists up. In cold weather water sometimes runs down the inside of windows.

4 Think through what is happening.

Water vapour is in the air all the time. It changes to liquid water when it is cooled. The air near the can is cooled. The mirror is cooler than the hot air in the bathroom.

KEY FACTS

water vapour – water in a gas form
condensation – the change from gas to liquid

 **Tip 1**

Use the correct word – 'condenses' rather than 'mists up'.

 Tip 2

Clouds are masses of tiny drops of liquid water that have condensed in the cold of the upper atmosphere.

Change of state

To achieve Level 5 you will need to know that materials can change state.
For example: liquids turn to solids when they cool. They turn to gases
when heated.

Let's practise!

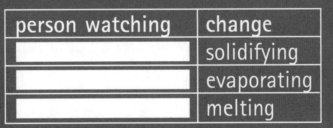

Question: Sam put some chocolate on a metal spoon. He held the spoon with a wooden peg. He heated the spoon over a candle flame. The chocolate melted and bubbled.

John dried a wet cloth on a hot radiator. He waited as the cloth dried.

Jane poured water from the tap into an ice cube maker and put it in the freezer for a day.

Which person watched the following changes of state?

Write their names in the correct place.

person watching	change
	solidifying
	evaporating
	melting

1. Read the question then read it again.

2. Remember the key facts.

3. Work through the problem.

You need to match the person to the change of state.

A liquid evaporates when it turns into a gas.
A liquid solidifies when it turns into a solid.
A solid melts when it turns into a liquid.

Now write in the name of the correct person.

KEY FACTS

liquid → **solidify** → solid   liquid → **evaporate** → gas   solid → **melt** → liquid

Separating mixtures

Achieved?

At Level 5 you will need to know about the ways to separate mixtures.
For example: mixtures where one part needs to be dissolved and then filtered.

Let's practise!

Question: Kate has been given a mixture of salt crystals and sand. She has been asked to separate the two solids. Describe how she should separate the solids.

1 Read the question then read it again.

It is a strange mixture but you need to get the two solids apart. Sieving won't help as the particles are about the same size and both would go through the sieve.

2 Remember the key facts.

Filters let liquids and dissolved solids through.

3 Work through the problem.

If you add water to the mixture, the salt will dissolve. The solution of salt and water will go through a filter but the sand will not.

4 Complete the experiment.

Let the water evaporate leaving the salt behind.

5 Think about other examples.

Other mixtures that could be separated in this way are sand and soap powder; sand and sugar. How would you separate:
- steel staples and sand?
- wax and sand?

Ways to separate mixtures:

sieve   use this to separate most undissolved solids from a liquid, or to separate two solids of different sizes

filter   use this to separate a solution from tiny undissolved pieces

KEY FACTS

dissolve – you cannot see the solid at all because it is in tiny particles in liquid

solution – a mixture where a solid has dissolved in a liquid

evaporate – this happens when a liquid turns to a gas. This leaves behind any dissolved solid

Metals

To achieve Level 5 you will need to know the main properties of metals.
For example: all metals conduct electricity and some are very heavy for their size.

Let's practise!

Question: Rey tested some materials. Two of the materials are metals. He made a table showing their properties.

Sample	Colour	Does it conduct electricity?	Heavy for size?
A	dark grey	yes	yes
B	white	no	no
C	silver	yes	no
D	green	no	no

Which are most likely to be metals?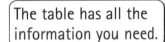

One of the metals is aluminium. The other is lead.

Aluminium is sample ☐ because...

Lead is sample ☐ because ...

① Read the question then read it again.

The table has all the information you need.

② Picture the question. What does it tell you?

Two of the samples conduct electricity. One of the samples conducts electricity AND is very heavy for its size.

③ Remember the key facts.

All metals conduct electricity. Aluminium is used to make aeroplanes.

④ Work through the problem.

Do the first part. Then decide which description matches lead best.

KEY FACTS

conducts electricity – lets electricity through

magnetic – attracted by a magnet

★ Tip

You don't need to know about the other two materials but they could be plastics of some kind.

Uses of metals

Achieved?

To achieve Level 5 you will need to know the main properties of metals.
For example: different metals are suited to different uses.

Let's practise!

Question: Use this table to answer the questions.

Metal	Is it expensive?	Does it rust?	Is it strong?	Is it magnetic?
steel	no	yes	yes	yes
gold	yes	no	no	no
platinum	yes	no	no	no
titanium	yes	no	yes	no

a) Which metals can be used to make expensive jewellery?

b) Motorcars need a strong body that is cheap. Which of these metals could be used to make cars?

c) Why would you not use titanium to make baked bean tins?

d) Which metal could be used to make compass needles?

1 Read the question then read it again.

2 What can you work out?

3 Study the table for clues.

4 Think about everyday examples.

Do one question at a time.

All the information is in the table.

Each metal has a different set of properties.

Look at the knives and forks you eat with. They are smooth and shiny. Look at the writing on them... it is almost certain to say 'stainless'. Most cars are made from steel that has been painted to stop it going rusty. Titanium is used for its great strength, but it is very expensive.

KEY FACTS

Metals are a very varied group of materials.

- Aluminium and titanium are very light.
- Gold and lead are very heavy.
- Lead and gold both melt at low temperatures.

- Tungsten is the metal in light bulb filaments. It melts only at very high temperatures.
- Steel cans are coated with a very thin layer of tin. Tin is an expensive metal.
- Rare metals like gold and platinum are used for jewellery.

Candle wax changes

To achieve Level 5 you will need to know about the properties of materials.

Let's practise!

Question: James lit a candle weighing 100 g. After an hour, he noticed that it had become smaller. The candle now weighed 60 g.

Explain why the candle weighs less after it has been burning for an hour.

What changes have taken place? Are these changes easy to reverse?

What will the candle be like in $1\frac{1}{2}$ hours time?

100 g   60 g

1) Read the question then read it again.

The candle weighs less after it has been burning – what has happened to the weight?

2) Picture the question. What does it tell you?

There is much less wax than there was. The wax must have been burnt.

3) Remember the key facts.

Wax burns and forms new materials. These new materials are gases.

4) Work through the problem.

Changes like this are difficult to reverse. This is an example of a chemical change.

SCIENCE BACKGROUND

When lighting a candle the match melts some wax. The wick soaks up the liquid wax which then evaporates off the wick. The wax gas then burns and makes new materials called carbon dioxide and water. Both these new materials are in the form of gases.

Wood burns and changes

Achieved?

To achieve Level 5 you will need to know the main properties of materials. For example: wood is a fuel. When it is burnt the wood is changed into new materials. These new materials cannot be turned back into wood.

Let's practise!

Question: On bonfire night the children saw a large pile of wood on fire. The next day they saw that the pile of wood was still smoking was much smaller.

 Matt thinks the wood had packed down.

 Julie thinks some of the wood changed into a gas when it was burnt.

 Hannah thinks that the wood had just turned to ash because of the heat.

a) Which of these children is correct?

b) Explain your idea.

1 Read the question then read it again.

2 Picture the question. What do you know?

3 Work through the problem.

The three children each have a different idea.

Burning wood is the same as burning candle wax. The wood is a fuel, just like the candle wax is the fuel for the candle.

When a fuel burns it changes into new materials. Many of these new materials are gases.

KEY FACT

Ash is the unburnt, solid part of the wood. It is a product of the fire. The weight of the ash left in the fire is much less than the weight of the wood they started with.

Circuit symbols

To achieve Level 5 you will need to know the symbols for electrical devices.
For example: the symbols for battery, bulb, switch and buzzer in a circuit.

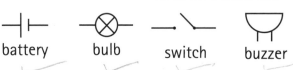

battery   bulb   switch   buzzer

Let's practise!

> **Question:** a) Draw two circuits that show two bulbs with a switch and a battery.
> - Draw one of the circuits with the switch open.
> - Draw the other circuit with the switch closed.
>
> b) Draw another circuit with a buzzer and two batteries.
> Practise drawing circuits here.

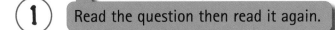

1 Read the question then read it again.

2 Picture the question.

3 Remember the key facts.

4 Work through the problem.

Draw a simple circuit with two bulbs and a battery.

Only use symbols. Do not use drawings.

A series circuit has the two bulbs arranged one after the other.

A switch is on when it looks like this.

It is off when it looks like this.

KEY FACTS

symbols – a way of showing an object with a very simple diagram that does not look like the real object

★ Tip

Always use a ruler when drawing circuit diagrams.

The size of forces

 Achieved?

To achieve Level 5 you will need to know about forces of different sizes.

Let's practise!

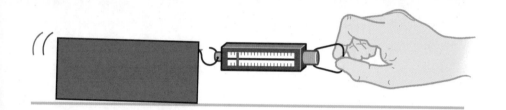

Question: Kim dragged a box across different surfaces. She used a Newton meter to measure the force.

She measured the force needed to move the box.

	Force needed to move box
On the level	16
Up a shallow slope	20
Up a steep slope	27

a) What units are used to measure force? _____

b) What was the only force Kim pulled against on a flat surface? _____

c) What forces was she pulling against on the slopes? _____

1 Read the question then read it again.

The question is in parts. Answer each part separately.

2 Picture the question. What do you know?

Think about a Newton meter. What are the units?

3 Remember the key facts.

The forces Kim is pulling against were gravity and friction. She was only pulling against friction on the flat surface.

KEY FACTS

force – a pull or push

friction – the force that tries to stop things moving against each other

newtons – the units used to measure force

gravity – the force which pulls all things together (e.g. us to the Earth and the Earth around the Sun)

Weighing in air and water

To achieve Level 5 you will need to be able to measure forces and explain the results. For example: the forces on an object in and out of water.

Let's practise!

Question: Paul weighed a brick using a force meter. He found it had a pull of 20 newtons. He dangled the brick into a bucket of water. He used the force meter to measure the pull. He found the pull was now only 14 newtons.

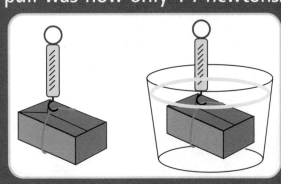

a) What force was pulling the brick down? _____

b) What force was helping to support the brick in water? _____

c) Why did it weigh less when it was hanging in water? _____

1 Read the question then read it again.

2 Picture the question.

3 Think of another example.

4 Remember the key facts.

The force pulling down pulls with a force of 20 newtons. There is another force that partly supports the brick when it is in water.

Draw the brick with arrows to show the direction of the forces pulling and pushing on it.

Normally you cannot lift up a person. In a swimming pool it is easy to support someone until you start to lift them out of the water.

Gravity is a force that pulls down. **Upthrust** from the water partly supports the weight of objects in water.

KEY FACTS

gravity – the force that pulls all objects towards the Earth

upthrust – the force that pushes up on objects in water

Air brakes

To achieve Level 5 you will need to know the names of forces and the direction they work in.
For example: air resistance is a force that works against the direction of movement.

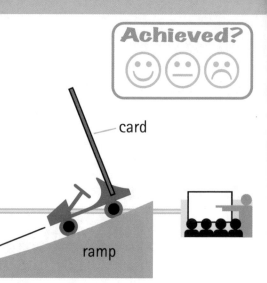
card

ramp

Let's practise!

Question: Ashleigh lets a toy car roll down a ramp. She measures how far it travels when it reaches level ground. She attaches a piece of card to the car. She changes the size of the card and measures how far the car goes each time. She calculates the area of each card. Explain the pattern of these results. Use the words 'air resistance' in your answer.

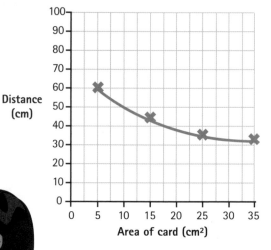

Distance (cm) vs Area of card (cm²)

1. Read the question then read it again.
2. Study the chart.
3. Remember the key facts.
4. Think of other examples.

The chart shows all the information you need.

The bigger the card, the less far the toy car went.

Air resistance is greater with a big area.

If you are running with a large sheet of cardboard, it is more difficult to run quickly if you hold it flat in front of you than if it is by your side.

KEY FACTS

Air resistance can only work on objects that are moving.

★ Tip

Try this experiment. It's easy to work out area if you use a square 'sail' each time made out of graph paper.

Pitch

To achieve Level 5 you will need to know some of the factors involved in the pitch of a sound.
For example: the tighter a string, the higher the pitch.

Let's practise!

Question: Meena is playing her violin. She experiments with the ways in which she can change the pitch of the sound.

a) She slackens a string.
What effect does that have on the pitch of the sound it makes when it is plucked?

_____

b) She puts her finger on the string to make it shorter.
What effect does that have on the pitch of the sound?

_____

c) Explain how the sound from the vibrating string reaches Meena's ears.

_____

(1) Read the question then read it again.

There are three parts to the question.

(2) Picture the question. What do you know?

The string vibrates. The quicker it vibrates, the higher the pitch.

(3) Remember the key facts.

- Tight strings have a high pitch.
- Slack strings have a low pitch.
- Short strings have a high pitch.
- Long strings have a low pitch.

(4) Think of similar examples.

- Small tuning forks are high pitched.
- Large tuning forks have a low pitch.
- Small (descant) recorders have a high pitch.
- Large (treble) recorders have a low pitch.

(5) Work through the problem.

Vibrating string makes the air vibrate and this travels through the air to her ear.

KEY FACTS

vibrate – something that moves backwards and forwards (or up or down)

pitch – the measure of how low or high a note is

How we see things

To achieve Level 5 you will need to know how light
is reflected off surfaces to reach our eyes.
For example: how light is bounced of mirrors.

Let's practise!

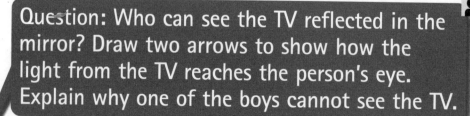
Question: Who can see the TV reflected in the mirror? Draw two arrows to show how the light from the TV reaches the person's eye. Explain why one of the boys cannot see the TV.

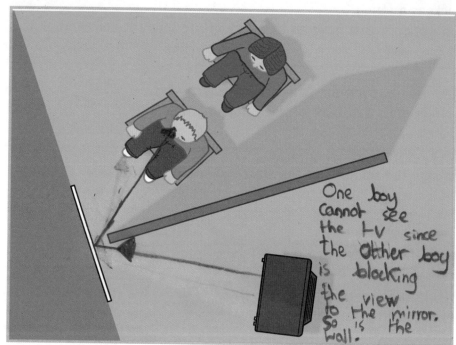

One boy cannot see the TV since the other boy is blocking the view to the mirror. So is the wall.

1) Read the question then read it again.

2) Remember the key facts.

3) Think about other examples.

You have to draw two arrows. Lines without arrowheads will not be enough.

The light comes from the source and hits the mirror. It then bounces off the mirror into the person's eye.

Light comes from a source and is reflected off this book into your eyes. Which is the main light source in your room now?

KEY FACTS

source – the object that gives off light

reflect – bounce off

Shadows and reflections

To achieve Level 5 you will need to know that light travels and bounces off objects.

Let's practise!

Question 1: Kim is looking at a book. Explain how she thinks the light is reflected so she can see the book.

Light reflects off the book and then the books reflected light goes into her eyes.

Question 2: Kim is trying to see the back of her head using mirrors. She thinks the light moves like this. Is she right? Explain your answer.

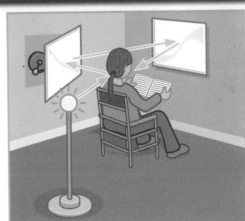

Yes, because her head is in a right angle to reflect light into a mirror.

(1) Read the question then read it again.

(2) Do something similar.

(3) Remember the key facts.

The first question is easier.

Try the experiment yourself using two mirrors.

Light travels and bounces off things. We see them when light from them enters our eye.

★ Tip

Play with two mirrors and make multiple reflections. This is how kaleidoscopes work.

Shadows

To achieve Level 5 you will need to know how shadows are formed.

Let's practise!

Question: Pat and Gary are making shadows using toy figures. They put a projector 1 metre from the wall and do not move it. Gary measures the distance that his toy is from the wall. He measures the height of the shadow made by the toy. The two boys draw a graph.

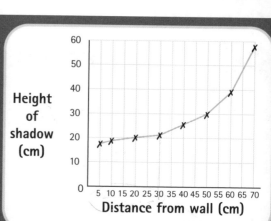

Height of shadow (cm)

Distance from wall (cm)

a) What was the size of the toy's shadow when it was 30 cm from the wall?

_21 cm._

b) What happens to the size of the toy's shadow as it gets further from the wall?

They size gets bigger

1 Read the question then read it again.

You only need to give one measurement to answer the first question. Now read the second question. You need to look for the pattern.

2 Picture the problem.

Draw a sketch of the projector, the toy and the wall. Try to draw it like a plan. Draw it with the toy very close to the wall and then again with it far away. This will help you work out in which position most light is blocked off. Now you can work out the pattern.

3 Look at the graph.

Put your finger on any point on the line on the graph. The bottom axis shows how far away the toy is from the wall. The side axis shows the size of the shadow.

4 Remember the key facts.

Shadows are made where light is cut off by an object. The size of the shadow gets bigger as the object gets further from the wall.

5 Check your answer.

The shadow can never be smaller than the toy.

The movement of the Sun

To achieve Level 5 you will need to know about the effects caused by the movement of the Earth.

Let's practise!

Question 1: Each day the Sun rises in the east and sets in the west. Explain why this happens.

① Read the question then read it again.

② Picture the question.

③ Remember the key facts.

Do not simply describe what happens. You should try to explain why.

Remember that you live on a huge turning ball. If you are looking south, then the Sun rises to your left. It sets to your right.

The Sun appears to move only because the Earth is turning on its axis.

Question 2: Sundials are used to help tell the time. Describe what happens to shadows from morning to noon to night.

① Picture the question.

② Remember the key facts.

Think of the shadows in your playground that you see at different times of day.

The Sun appears to move across the sky, but it is the Earth that turns. When the Sun rises it is low in the sky and shadows are long. During the day it rises higher and shadows become shorter. Past midday the Sun gets lower in the sky. The shadows become longer again.

KEY FACTS

midday – middle of the day (noon)

Sun – the star that gives us heat and light

axis – an imaginary stick through the Earth around which it rotates

The year

At Level 5 you should be able to describe the movement of the Earth.
For example: the Earth's orbit movement that gives us a year.

Let's practise!

Question: This diagram shows the Earth and Sun. Add an arrow to show the way the Earth orbits the Sun. How long does it take the Earth to make half a complete orbit of the Sun?

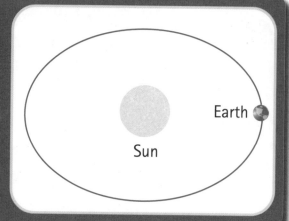

Sun

Earth

1 Read the question then read it again.

Draw the arrow showing the orbit of the Earth around the Sun. Do not confuse this with the way the Earth spins on its own axis.

2 Picture the question.

The orbit of the Earth is around the Sun. In this picture, you are looking down on the Earth from above the north pole.

3 Remember the key facts.

The Sun is actually moving, but for this question we imagine that it stays still. The Earth spins on its axis and orbits the Sun, along with eight other planets.

4 Work through the problem.

The Earth takes one year to orbit the Sun.

5 Check your answer.

It takes the Earth six months to get halfway around its orbit.

KEY FACTS

orbit – to move around another object

spin – to turn on its own axis

year – the time taken for a planet to make a complete orbit of the Sun

★ Tip

The Earth orbits the Sun in an anticlockwise direction.

A year on the planet Mercury is only 88 days long because it is much closer to the Sun and its orbit is shorter. Further from the Sun = longer year.

Predicting

To achieve Level 5 you will need to use results of experiments to help predict what is likely to happen.
For example: you should use a line graph to predict how quickly sugar will dissolve in water of a particular temperature.

Let's practise!

Question:

a) What does this line graph tell you about the way sugar dissolves in water?

The hotter temperature, the faster the sugar dizzolves.

b) How long do you think it will take the sugar to dissolve in water at 70°C?

40 seconds

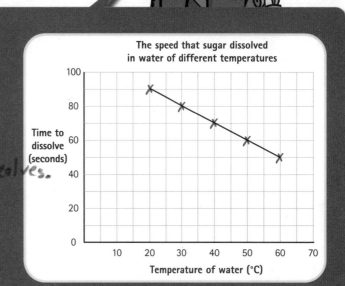

The speed that sugar dissolved in water of different temperatures

Time to dissolve (seconds)

Temperature of water (°C)

(1) Read the question then read it again.

You need to use the information on the graph.

(2) Picture the question. What does it tell you?

The time taken for sugar to dissolve depends on the temperature of the water.

(3) Think about everyday examples.

Sugar dissolves quickly in hot tea but takes a long time to dissolve in a cold drink.

(4) Work through the problem for a).

Look along the bottom of the graph until you reach 60°C. Go straight up until you hit the line. Look across to the number on the side axis.

(5) Work through the problem for b).

Continue the graph line downwards until it reaches the line above 70°C. Look across to the number on the side axis.

KEY FACTS

dissolve – mix a solid and a liquid until you cannot see the solid at all
temperature – a measure of how hot something is

Explaining results

Achieved?

☺ ☺ ☹

To reach Level 5 you will need to be able to explain the results of tests.

Let's practise!

Question: Sami and Leon made parachutes of different sizes and attached a weight to them. They used the same weight each time. They tested how long it took the parachutes to fall from the same height. Here are their results:

Size of the parachute (cm²)	Drop 1	Drop 2	Drop 3	Average (seconds)
400	3.1	3.2	3.1	3.1
300	2.9	2.9	3.2	3.0
200	2.6	2.6	2.6	2.6
100	2.4	2.6	2.5	2.5

a) Why did Sami and Leon do each test three times?

To make sure the answer was correct

b) What was the average time taken for the 200 cm² parachute to fall?

2.6 seconds

c) Explain the pattern of these results.

The more size, the longer the drop.

d) Draw a line graph using the size and average.

① Read the question then read it again.

② Remember the key facts.

③ Work through the problem.

The answer is in the table.
The final column is an average.

Air resistance slows objects that move through the air. The bigger the object, the more air resistance there is.

They did the test three times to check that their results were reliable. The average for the 200 cm² parachute was 2.6 seconds. The bigger the parachute, the slower it fell. This is because there is more air resistance acting on a bigger parachute.

KEY FACTS

average – you work out the mean (a type of average) by adding the times for each drop and dividing by the number of drops

air resistance – the force that tries to stop objects that are moving through the air

Using evidence to reach a conclusion

To reach Level 5 you will need to use evidence to reach a conclusion.
For example: making connections between sets of information.

Let's practise!

Question: Ali and Louise looked for minibeasts in different habitats. They made a table of results.

Place	In the soil of the flower bed	Under the hedge	Under stones	On the rose bushes
Type	Damp soil	Dry soil	Damp & dark	Bright & sunny
greenfly	0	0	0	34
worms	4	0	6	0
spiders	1	2	1	2
ants	0	lots	0	3
slugs	1	0	4	0

Tick the correct conclusions.

a) Worms live in dry places. ☐

b) Spiders are not adaptable and can only be found in one habitat. ☐

c) Slugs can live in damp places. ☑

d) It is too dry under the hedge for anything to live there. ☐

e) Ants eat greenfly. ☐

Add a correct conclusion of your own.

1 Read the question then read it again.

2 Picture the question. What does it tell you?

3 Remember the key facts.

4 Work through the problem.

Look at the table. Think about which animals like to live where.

The children looked in four different places for minibeasts.

Try to use only the evidence from the table and do not add anything you think you know about these minibeasts.

Tick the correct conclusions.

KEY FACTS

habitat – place where an animal or plant lives

adapted – special feature which makes it better at surviving in an environment

environment – the conditions of a habitat (e.g. temperature and moisture)

Evaluating experiments

Achieved?

To reach Level 5 you will need to be able to say whether your experiments were good ones.
For example: you should be able to suggest ways in which experiments could be improved.

Let's practise!

Question: Rashid is experimenting with a simple elastic car launcher. He pulls back the same distance each time. He measured how far his toy red and blue cars travelled on different surfaces.
Rashid said: "My results show that cars travel further on a wood floor."

	carpet	wood floor
red car	30 cm	33 cm
blue car	40 cm	41 cm

a) How could Rashid improve his test?

Get another   surface

b) Are his conclusions reliable?

No because he didn't mention the blue car being faster.

1 Read the question then read it again.

Do you think he did enough tests? Did he need to work out an average? Do his results look believable?

2 Picture the question. What does it tell you?

He only did each test once. He thinks that the wood floor is best because both cars went further.

3 Study the table.

The distance travelled by the blue car was only a little further on the wood floor.

4 Remember the key facts.

Try to repeat readings if possible so that you have an average for each surface and each car.

5 Check your answer.

Rashid should have done more tests and worked out an average to check his results.

★ Tip

Always repeat measurements.

Make sure the results really support your conclusion.

KEY FACTS

Reliable experiments are those that give results that you can trust.

Using line graphs to make predictions

To achieve Level 5 you will need to be able to interpret line graphs.
For example: this line graph shows the time that a candle burns in jars of different sizes.

Let's practise!

Question:

a) How long would the candle burn for in a jar of 250 ml?
15 seconds

b) How long would you expect it to burn for in a jar of 600 ml?
36 seconds

c) Is it true that a candle will burn twice as long in a jar that has twice the volume? Explain your answer using what you know about burning things in air.
Yes, a flame needs air.

d) Do candles burn three times as long in jars with three times the volume?
Yes, 3 times more air.

e) Which are the two variables in this experiment?
Size and time.

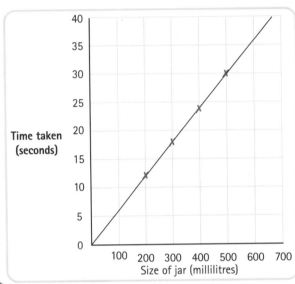

(1) Read the question then read it again.

(2) Picture the question. What does it tell you?

(3) Study the last question.

(4) Remember the key facts.

Look at the graph. It shows a steady increase in the length of time that the candle will burn for.

The candle in the jar uses up the air. Bigger jars contain more air than smaller jars.

The two variables are the things that change. We alter the size of the jar as the time it burns for depends on jar size.

Candles burn the wax. They need air to do this. The jar fills up with the gases given off by the burning wax.

aking sense of graphs

To reach Level 5 you will need to be able to draw and interpret line graphs.

Let's practise!

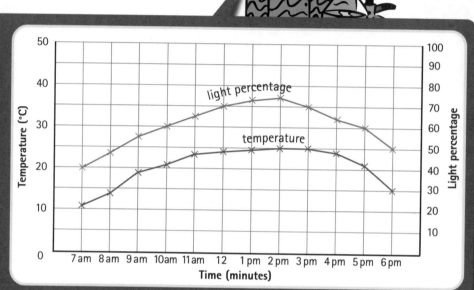

Experiment: Class 6 left sensors switched on all day in their classroom. They used:

- a temperature sensor
- a light sensor.

a) Tell the story of the temperature in the classroom during the day. *The temperature increased throughout the day, then decreased.*

b) Tell the story of the light in the classroom during the day. *The light got brighter, then slowly coming to 6pm decreased*

c) Does it look like the lights were turned on during the day? Explain your answer. *Yes because the sun was bright in the window, this gave the effect.*

① Read the question then read it again.

② Picture the question. What does it tell you?

③ Remember the key facts.

Make sure you read the correct line against the correct verticle axis.

The lines tell the story of the day. When was the room warmest and brightest?

Computer sensors help record the data and draw the graph. Your job is to make sense of the lines they draw.

A last idea

Computer sensors are very useful in recording events in the environment. Some places round your school have a wide range of temperatures and others have steadier temperatures. The sensors would be able to tell the story of each place without you having to go there every hour.

KEY FACTS – Sc1

At Level 4 you need to be able to:

★ see that you need evidence to support scientific ideas

★ decide on the best way to do an experiment or test

★ make good predictions

★ select the most important information

★ choose the best equipment for a test

★ record observations and measurements

★ draw and make sense of a bar chart

★ come to conclusions

★ say ways in which work can be improved

At Level 5 you need to be able to:

★ explain scientific ideas

★ choose the best information

★ choose the right equipment to make measurements

★ use the equipment correctly

★ repeat measurements

★ explain why there might be differences between measurements of the same thing

★ understand line graphs

★ draw line graphs

★ suggest ways in which work could be improved

★ use scientific ways to communicate ideas

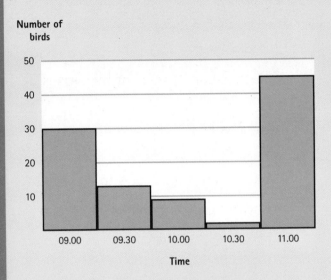

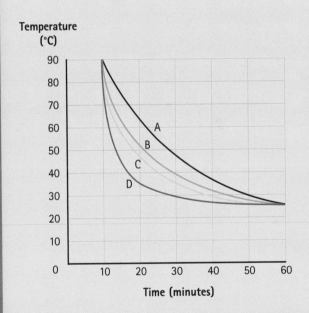

KEY FACTS – Sc2

At Level 4 you need to know:

★ the names of some of the organs of the human body

★ the position of some of the organs of the human body

★ the names and position of some of the organs of a variety of plants

★ how to use simple keys to identify living things

★ how to put living things into groups

★ about food chains

At Level 5 you need to know:

★ the jobs done by some of the organs in the human body

★ the jobs done by some of the organs in plants

★ about the life cycles of humans and some other animals

★ about the life cycles of plants

★ how to classify some living things

★ that living things are found in places that suit them

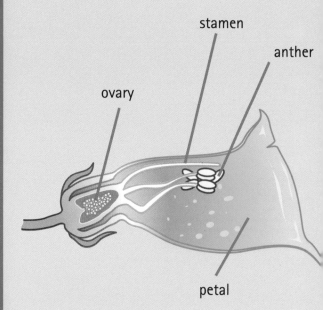

stamen

anther

ovary

petal

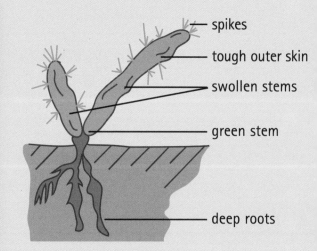

spikes

tough outer skin

swollen stems

green stem

deep roots

KEY FACTS - Sc3

At Level 4 you need to know:

★ about the properties of materials

★ how materials are classified into solids, liquids and gases

★ how to separate simple mixtures

★ the scientific words used to describe changes, such as condense, evaporate and freeze

★ which changes are easily reversed and which changes are difficult to reverse

At Level 5 you need to know:

★ the properties of metals

★ the ways in which metals differ from other solids

★ the ways in which changes, such as evaporation and condensation, take place

★ how to separate mixtures of materials

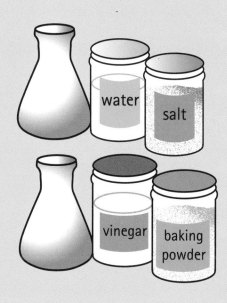

KEY FACTS - Sc4

At Level 4 you need to know:

★ how to alter electrical circuits

★ how the Sun changes position during the day

★ that objects are attracted by gravity

★ which things are attracted by magnets

★ magnets can attract and repel each other

★ how shadows are formed

★ that sounds travel through a variety of materials

At Level 5 you need to know:

★ how to alter the current flowing in a circuit

★ about the effect of adding bulbs to a series circuit

★ about the effects of adding and subtracting batteries from a circuit

★ how to measure forces

★ that forces operate in particular directions

★ how to draw circuits using symbols

★ how to change the pitch and loudness of a sound

★ that vibrations result in sounds

★ that the light from objects passes into your eyes

★ about the orbit of the Earth and the Moon

★ how to use knowledge of orbits to explain the length of the day and year

battery

bulb

switch

buzzer

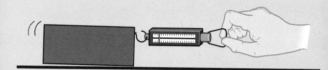

ANSWERS

Page 10
a) The shoots without any roots.
b) The seedlings with most roots would grow best.

Page 11
Heat must travel through the metal, wood and plastic. The hotter object must be made of a good thermal conductor. Polystyrene is a very poor conductor.

Page 12
They let the water from the solutions evaporate and leave just the sugar.

Page 13
Sara is right because friction is stopping the wheelbarrow from moving. It cannot be air resistance as that acts only when something is moving.

Page 14
The compass needle is very delicately balanced and moves easily when the repelling magnet is near.
The red and blue poles are unlike. Unlike magnetic poles attract.
Both red poles are alike. Like magnetic poles repel.
Both blue poles are alike. Like poles repel.

Page 15
Iron and steel are the metals that are magnetic.

Page 16
Brown is the most common eye colour.

Page 17
The amount of force needed to break the strips depends on the type of paper.
Approximate answers are:
Tissue paper – less than 25N
Kitchen towel – less than 50N
Newspaper – less than 75N
Carrier bag – the same amount of force
Writing paper – less than 75N

Page 18
a) The pattern of results shows that the ping pong ball is the best bouncer.
b) 56 cm was a mistake.
c) It was higher than the others even though the tennis ball was usually worst.

Page 19
Shefqat – compost/temperature
Julie – type of exercise
Tim – all

Page 20
Heart pumps blood around the body. This carries oxygen to all parts of the body.
Lungs are the place where gases are exchanged between the air and the body.
Stomach begins digestion.

Page 21
1 Ovary – holds the seeds or ovules.
2 Stigma – the female part of the flower that gathers in the pollen.
3 Stamen – produces the pollen.
4 Petal – Attracts insects to the flower which then pollinate the flower and protects the underside of the flower.

Page 22
Katy is right.
Sanjay missed out the fact that the blood goes back to the heart before going out to the body again.
Jake missed out the fact that after the blood comes from the body it goes back to the heart before going to the lungs.

Page 23
The girl's heart rate goes up for one minute, then stays at 90 beats per minute for 5 minutes. She then exercised harder and her pulse went up to 120 beats per minute. The heart beats faster when the body needs more oxygen and sugar for energy – if it is exercising. It drops back down when the person stops exercising.

Page 24
Eggs – the fly starts as an egg. These are laid outside the mother fly's body.
Maggot – the fly is born from the egg as a maggot.
Pupa – The maggot makes a covering around itself while it changes into an adult fly.
Adult – the fly emerges from the pupa as an adult. It lays eggs and dies.

Page 25
1 Germination of seed
2 Growing plant
3 Flowering
4 Pollination
5 Development of seeds
6 Dispersal of seeds

Page 26
A – oak
B – chestnut

Page 27
Mammal – whale, kangaroo / gives birth to live young and feeds young on milk
Bird – swallow, sparrow / has feathers and lays eggs
Reptile – alligator, lizard / has dry scaly skin and lays eggs on land
Amphibian – toad, newt / has damp skin and lays eggs in water
Fish – cod, stickleback / lives in water and has gills

Page 28
Woodlice are small animals that need damp and dark conditions. They feed on rotting plants. Worms like damp soil and they eat leaves and vegetation which falls on the ground. Slugs and snails like green vegetables and carrots. Spiders will need something to hang their web from.

Page 29
Tough outer skin to stop water evaporating.
Spikes to stop animals eating the plant.
Deep roots to get water from the soil.
Green stem to make food.
Swollen stems to store water.

Page 30
Before the trees have leaves there is enough light, water and minerals for the small plants beneath them. Once the leaves come out the tree blocks out the light and uses most of the water and minerals. Evergreens block the light all year round making the ground bare.

Page 31
Melt then burn – chocolate,
Burn without melting – wood, bread, wool
No change – salt

Page 32
The salt dissolved in the water.
Baking powder and vinegar are making a gas.
Mixing vinegar with baking soda.

Page 33
With a fan the evaporated water is blown away, allowing more water to evaporate, so blowing across the liquid makes evaporation faster.

Page 34
Water vapour changed to liquid water when it cooled down. When the air near the cold can cooled, water vapour in the air formed as drips on
the can. The can which was already at room temperature did not make water vapour condense.

Page 35
Solidify – Jane; Evaporate – John; Melt – Sam

Page 36
Kate dissolved the salt in water. She then filtered the sand and salt solution and then let the water evaporate, leaving the salt behind.

Page 37
C and A. Aluminium is sample C. Lead is sample A.

Page 38
Stainless steel. Steel and aluminium. It is strong and light. Because it is too expensive.
a) Gold and platinum can be made into jewellery
b) Cars are made of steel
c) Titanium is too expensive
d) Steel is the only magnetic material in the list

Page 39
Because some of the candle has melted, reacted with oxygen in the air and made new gases.
The wax burned and gas was released. This is a chemical change which is difficult to reverse. The candle will have all burnt away.

Page 40
Julie. When a fuel burns it produces new materials. These new materials are gases.

Page 41

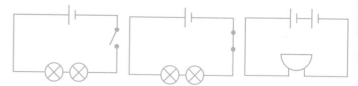

Page 42
a) Newtons
b) Friction and gravity
c) Friction

Page 43
a) Gravity
b) Upthrust
c) It weighed less because upthrust force was supporting the brick in the water.

Page 44
The results actually show that the larger the card, the less distance the car travelled. This is because air resistance slowed it down.

Page 45
a) It lowered the pitch of the sound.
b The pitch is higher with a shorter string.
c) The vibrations in the string vibrate the air and this vibration travels to Meena's ear.

Page 46

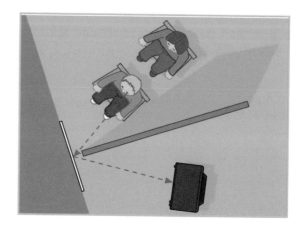

Page 47
1) Light from the Sun reflected from the book into Kim's eye.
2) Light hit the back of Kim's head. It bounced off her head onto the mirror, then onto the other mirror. It then bounced off that mirror into her eye.

Page 48
a) 22 cm. b) The size of the shadow gets bigger as it gets further from the wall.

Page 49
1) The Sun appears to rise in the east when you look because the Earth is rotating anti-clockwise on its axis.
2) During the day, the Sun appears to rise in the sky and therefore the shadows are shorter. In the afternoon, the Sun appears to get lower and the shadows get longer again.

Page 50
Arrow should show anti-clockwise direction of the Earth's orbit.
6 months or half a year, or 182/183 days.

Page 51
a) The warmer the water, the faster the sugar dissolves.
b) 40 seconds

Page 52
a) To check their results were reliable.
b) 2.6 seconds
c) The bigger the parachute, the slower it fell because more air resistance was acting on the bigger parachute.
d)

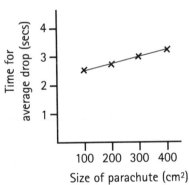

Page 53
Correct conclusions: c) slugs can live in damp places.

Page 54
a) He could do each test more than once to improve the reliability; he could test more surfaces; he could test more cars.
b) Not really, because the results were not different enough.

Page 55
a) 14–16 seconds
b) 36–37 seconds
c) Yes, because there is more air to burn in a bigger jar. The graph shows the time doubles when the jar size doubles.
d) This is true.
e) The variables are size of jar and time it burns.

Page 56
a) The temperature started at 12°C. It gradually increases to 25°C at 2pm. It stayed the same until 3pm and then began to cool off until it was 15°C at 6pm.
b) The light gradually increased until 2pm when it began to get less bright.
c) No – the light doesn't suddenly change.

Notes